I0555306

Rhett's Wonderful World

By
Rafe Underwood Butler

Copyrights © 2025

All rights reserved

Library of Congress Control Number: 2025921427

ISBN:

978-1-966355-41-0

Dedication

To my son, Rhett Butler

From the moment you arrived, you taught me that communication comes in many forms, and that love does not depend on words alone. You prove to me every single day that progress isn't about speed or comparison, but about growth that is true to who you are. I have watched you move through life with patience, curiosity, and a bravery that often speaks louder than any sentence ever could.

You progress every day in the most personal, meaningful ways. Sometimes it's a new gesture or sign you use to tell me what you need, sometimes it's the way you hold my gaze a little longer, or the way you choose a familiar routine and see it through with quiet determination. Other days, it's the way a favorite song or activity sparks a glow in your eyes, or how you navigate a transition with growing calm. These moments small or shining are milestones that remind me how capable you are and how much you have to teach me about patience, presence, and joy.

Your daily progress fills our home with hope. It teaches me to listen more deeply, to celebrate every step, and to trust in your unique rhythm of growth. You have shown me that strength can be gentle, that resilience can be quiet, and that love, in its purest form, is unwavering. I am endlessly proud of you for who you are and for how you grow into yourself with honesty, resilience, and an open heart.

This book is dedicated to you, my incredible son. Thank you for being my daily inspiration and for filling my life with purpose, wonder, and an immeasurable amount of love. I am so proud of you, and I love you more than words can say.

With all my love,

Rafe Butler

Acknowledgement

Rhett's Wonderful World would not be the same without the love, encouragement, and inspiration from those who have stood by us and shaped Rhett's life. To Grandfather Ron Butler, Grandmother Beverly Underwood, Mother Eliza Schroeder, Grandmother Vicki Schroeder, Grandfather Bill Schroeder, Step-grandfather Sid Butler, Aunt Katie Burton, Uncle John Burton, and Cousin Camron thank you for being in Rhett's life and for helping us in every way possible with Rhett Butler. Your presence, support, and love have made this book possible and have filled Rhett's world with wonder and joy.

With heartfelt gratitude, Rafe Butler

In a lively town filled with colors and sounds, where the air often carried the sweet scent of freshly baked bread from the bakery, lived a boy named Rhett. Rhett was special, just like a rainbow after a rainstorm. He had bright blue eyes that sparkled with curiosity and a smile that could light up even the darkest day, making it feel as if the clouds had never been there at all.

Rhett loved many things: the feel of soft blankets wrapped snugly around him on chilly mornings, the sound of birds chirping in the early light, and the taste of chocolate chip cookies fresh from the oven with their sweet aroma filling the air and the chocolate melting softly on his tongue. But most of all, he loved to explore the wonderful world with his wide-eyed curiosity and a heart eager for adventure.

Every morning, Rhett would put on his favorite red cap, as if it were a part of him, and grab his trusty backpack filled with all the things he cherished. Inside, he kept his special notebook on which he drew everything he discovered, liked, and loved, things he wanted to keep close to him. Each page of his notebook was filled with amazing pictures from his imagination and adventures.

One sunny day, Rhett woke up. Snuggled in his blanket, he decided to visit the park. As he walked along the path, he noticed the flowers dancing in the breeze, their petals swaying gently as if they were waving him hello. "Look at the daisies!" he exclaimed, his voice bubbling with excitement.

Mesmerized by the view, Rhett started sketching the bright yellow faces of the flowers in his notebook, while the soft fragrance of the blooms drifted around him.

While Rhett was drawing the daisies in his notebook at the park, he saw children playing and laughing. Their quick movements and bursts of laughter all seemed to rush toward him at once, filling the space with more energy than he was ready for.

Sometimes, it felt a bit overwhelming for him, as if all the colors in the world had spilled onto his canvas, all at once. But he remembered his breathing exercises, taking deep breaths in and out, and feeling the cool breeze brush against his cheeks, just like the gentle swaying of the trees.

As he walked around the park, Rhett spotted a little girl sitting alone on a swing, her feet barely touching the ground. Rhett was very shy at first, but he also wanted to play with someone. Thus, he gathered his courage, walked towards her, and asked gently, "*Hi! My name is Rhett. Would you like to play with me?*"

The girl, with big black eyes and golden hair that gently swayed back and forth with each movement of the swing, smiled and nodded. Her eyes lit up with surprise, and together they swung high into the sky; the wind rushing past their faces as they giggled with joy.

After swinging for a little while, they jumped off and wandered into a field full of flowers, each one bright and colorful.

As they played, Rhett showed her one of his drawings. *"This is a rocket ship!"* he said excitedly, pointing to the tall rocket he drew, with a shiny pointy top and bright flames coming from the bottom.

The girl's eyes sparkled, *"Wow, can we make a rocket ship together?"* she asked, her voice filled with excitement. And so, they began to create a magical world of imagination, drawing their rocket on paper and pretending it could fly above the clouds.

Soon, as the day began to fade, it was time for the girl to go. She waved goodbye with a big smile, and Rhett waved back, feeling happy for the new friend he had made.

While thinking about the new friend he made, he learned that everyone has unique gifts. Some could run faster than the wind. Some could sing beautifully like the birds. And some, like Rhett, who could see the world in a special way, noticing little things such as the rain falling softly from the sky, the clouds making different shapes, the tiny ants marching in a line, or the rainbow colors sparkling in a puddle, things that others might miss, but Rhett could see.

As the clouds started to cover the sky, Rhett returned home, tired but happy. He kicked off his shoes and went straight to his favorite spot by the window. Opening his notebook, he drew a picture of the park, with trees, bright flowers, and the little girl he had met that day, playing in the middle of it all. Rhett knew his wonderful world was full of possibilities, and he was excited for tomorrow's adventures.

As he drifted off to sleep, Rhett smiled, dreaming of colorful rainbows, his new friend who made him happy, and the amazing journey of being himself. In Rhett's world, being different was something to celebrate; things such as going to the park, making new friends, and showing his treasured pictures. Just as the moon makes the sky special, all these things made Rhett's day magical.

Rhett's story aims to emphasize the beauty of uniqueness and the importance of friendship, encouragement, understanding, and acceptance. It shows that everyone sees the world in their own way, and it's those differences that make us special.

Through his eyes, we discover how simple moments like doing what you love, meeting someone new, and sharing a part of yourself can fill our hearts with joy. And when we truly accept and celebrate one another, we create a world that feels warmer, kinder, and full of love for everyone.

The Parenting Journey

Parenting an autistic child is a journey filled with unique challenges, profound joys, and everything in between. It is a path that has always and will always require patience, resilience, and a deep commitment to understanding a child's unique way of experiencing the world.

During this journey, the highs can be incredibly rewarding, offering moments of pride, joy, and connection that are unmatched, while the lows can test emotional and physical endurance.

For families, walking this emotional journey means facing constant shifts as their child's needs and behaviors change. It also demands the ability to respond and adapt in real time to changes in a child's needs, behaviors, and communication.

These shifts can occur daily or even hourly, requiring parents to always remain attentive. In doing so, families learn to balance the challenges with the moments of joy, building a foundation of acceptance, love, and understanding.

Remember, children with autism see the world in their own beautiful ways, and with love and patience, that world can grow into something truly wonderful for them. Our job is to only walk beside them, guiding, supporting, and celebrating every step they take on their unique journey.

The Emotional Rollercoaster

When parents first receive the news of their child's autism diagnosis, it often leads to a whirlpool of emotions. Initially, there may be a sense of shock or even grief as they process what this means for their child's future. The expectations they had for "normal" milestones, such as speaking their first words or making friends, might suddenly seem out of reach, and it's common for parents to go through stages of denial, anger, and eventually acceptance.

Yet, as they learn more about autism, many parents also discover a whole new world of joy. They start to appreciate and celebrate the unique perspectives their child offers, often developing a deeper bond. The joy of witnessing their child's special interests or talents, whether it's a knack for music, mathematics, or art, can be immensely rewarding. And it's moments like these that serve as precious reminders of their child's individuality and the beauty of diversity.

Daily Challenges

Daily life with an autistic child can be both challenging and unpredictable. Parents often face communication barriers as their child may struggle to express their thoughts or feelings verbally. This can lead to frustration for both the parents and the child, especially during difficult situations such as when the child is throwing tantrums or having meltdowns. Furthermore, navigating social situations can also be daunting, as children may not naturally understand cues from peers, leading to feelings of isolation, both for them and their parents.

That's why making and following a routine is essential for many autistic children, since they often find themselves establishing structured schedules, as it provides a sense of security to them.

Changes in routine, however, can result in anxiety for the child, leading to more stress for the family. Unexpected changes in school schedules, loud or crowded environments, or sudden transitions between activities can be particularly difficult to manage.

Moreover, sensory overload from bright lights, strong smells, or excessive noise can also disrupt their sense of calm, making everyday outings or social events challenging. Parents may also encounter societal ignorance or a lack of understanding, which can add to their feelings of isolation and frustration.

Practical Obstacles

There are significant practical obstacles on this journey as well, such as managing the educational system, finding appropriate therapies, and securing support services. As an autistic child prepares to begin school, securing the right school placement, ensuring teachers understand the child's needs, and coordinating with multiple professionals can be overwhelming for parents who are already managing day-to-day challenges.

Many parents become advocates for their child, attending Individualized Education Program (IEP) meetings and seeking out specialized programs, which can be time-consuming and emotionally taxing.

Additionally, financial strain is a common hurdle. The costs of therapies, special schooling, and medical bills can accumulate quickly, leading to stress and anxiety. Moreover, transportation to appointments, time away from work, and the need for adaptive equipment can add further pressure.

Some families are blessed with a strong support network, while others find themselves feeling overwhelmed and alone, often having to navigate this demanding journey with little outside help or understanding.

Coping Mechanisms

Given these challenges, parents must develop coping mechanisms to handle the inevitable stress and emotional upheaval. Start with self-care, that's. Finding time for personal interests, hobbies, and relaxation can recharge parents and prevent burnout. Regular exercise, walking, yoga, or team sports can significantly improve mental and physical well-being.

Then there are support networks of other parents, which can provide immeasurable comfort. Sharing experiences, seeking advice, and simply knowing that you are not alone can help parents feel more secure. Online communities and local support groups can strip away feelings of isolation and encourage connection.

Professional support, such as therapy or counseling, can also be beneficial. Speaking with a licensed therapist can provide parents with valuable tools to manage their feelings and navigate the difficulties they face. Mindfulness techniques and stress-reduction strategies, like meditation or journaling, can help maintain mental clarity and emotional stability.

Happy Moments and Positives

Amidst all the challenges, it's the happy moments that truly stand out. Parents often find joy in the small victories, the first time their child engages in a conversation, enjoys a new activity, or accomplishes a goal, no matter how minor. Celebrations of special interests, like attending a concert for a favorite band or visiting a museum for a specific exhibition, bring excitement and happiness.

Parents of autistic children frequently develop a greater sense of resilience and empathy, both for their child and for others facing difficulties. This experience cultivates a deep appreciation for life's moments; however small they may be. The laughter shared during family activities, the pride in their child's uniqueness, and the fulfillment that comes from supporting their growth and discoveries create a richly rewarding parenting experience.

Conclusion:

In conclusion, being a parent to an autistic child is an intricate journey filled with ups and downs. Although the path can be fraught with obstacles, it is also rich with joy, love, and an unparalleled bond that flourishes through understanding and acceptance.

During this journey, the skills parents learn and the resilience they build prove invaluable, shaping them not only as caregivers but also as advocates, teachers, and lifelong learners. Embracing this journey is about celebrating each moment, recognizing the beauty in differences, and nurturing their child's unique gifts and potential. Through the challenges, they find strength, joy, and ultimately, an abiding love that knows no bounds. And in the quiet moments, a shared smile, a gentle hug, or a small victory hard-won, they are reminded that this love is the greatest gift of all.

A Love Like No Other

In the stillness of night, when the stars softly gleam,

A whisper of love flows as I pause and I dream.

You entered my world, a bright spark, a gift,

In ways I couldn't fathom, my heart you uplift.

Each morning, we rise to a canvas anew,

With colors of laughter, and shades of the blue.

Your laughter ignites like the sun breaking free,

It dances through rooms, a melody of glee.

Yet in moments of silence, I sense the weight,

Of challenges looming that we learn to navigate.

The world feels so big, where chaos can reign,

When the sounds become storms, and it drives you to pain.

With every "why" that echoes in our space,

I strive to find answers, to keep up the pace.

In crowded places, your hand grips so tight,

You search for my presence, your comfort each night.

Meltdowns like thunder can shatter our calm,

And I hold you through storms, with whispers of balm.

When the world feels too heavy, and you've lost your way,

I promise I'm here, come what may, come what may.

But oh, the little victories, how they shine like bright stars,

When you conquer a fear or share your own scars.

Each milestone we celebrate your triumphs, my dear,

These are the treasures of parenting that bring me such cheer.

Through art and expression, you teach me to see,

The world through your lens, rich in mystery.

The endless connections, in patterns and play,

Reveal a great wisdom that brightens my day.

In our journey, we've met friends who understand,

With warm hearts that open and lend us a hand.

Together we grow, sharing stories and tears,

Building a family that conquers our fears.

There are days filled with doubt, when I'm feeling so low,

Wondering if I'll find the strength to bestow.

Yet your smile reminds me of the light that we share,

Of the love that unites us, of the bond that we bear.

So, here's to the struggles, the laughter, the tears,

To the lessons we learn over countless years.

For being your parent is a ride unlike others,

Where love holds us close, like a blanket, it covers.

In the tapestry of life, we weave day by day,

Creating our story in our own special way.

Though challenges linger and shadows may fall,

In the heart of our journey, together, we stand tall.

You are my warrior, my teacher, my son,

In this vast world together, we shine like the sun.

Through ups and through downs, in joy and in strife,

Being your parent is the love of my life.

www.ingramcontent.com/pod-product-compliance
Lightning Source LLC
Chambersburg PA
CBHW041434120626
46547CB00002B/217